Out of Doors. Nature Songs

OUT OF DOORS

Out of Doors
NATURE
SONGS

ANNIE JOHNSON FLINT

Author of
"By the Way"
"Songs of the Blessed Hope"
"Songs of Faith and Comfort"
"Songs of Grace and Glory"
"Songs of the Saviour"
"Songs in the Night"

Uniform in Style and Price
Copyrighted

Evangelical Publishers
———Incorporated 1912———
366 Bay Street - Toronto 2, Canada

Printed in Canada by

In The Beginning

THE lights of the city gleam and glow
    In the misty purple dusk,
    Bursting out of the grimy globes
Like tropical fruits from the husk:
A myriad sparkling orbs of light,—
Violet, golden, scarlet, white,—
    Blazing up at the stars of night.

But the light was not in the globes;
    Man's hand has led it there,
His power, his thought, the wonder wrought,
    Captured and chained the flare;
And the light obeys his will,
    The mind of man and his skill.

But back of the light is the power house,
    Where the great wheels tireless turn,
Where the pulleys lift and the gearings shift,
    And the roaring fires burn.
And back of the power the mine,
    Where the toiling slaves of the Lamp
Burrow like moles in the black pit-holes
    In the dust and the deadly damp.

And back of the mine are the buried trees
    Where the strong winds laid them low,
Charred by the fires of centuries,
    Smoldering deep and slow;
The days of the Lord are a thousand years,
    The eves and the morns of the circling spheres,
And a thousand thousand lingering days
    Passed over the trees and the hidden blaze.

And back of the charred trees are the green,
  When the columnar shafts rose high;
And back of the forest the white-hot sun,
  With its cords of the heat and the moisture spun
Drawing the seedlings out of the earth,
  Up and up to the sky.

And back of the sun is the Voice, that spoke
  Unto the light, and the light awoke;
From the dateless dawning of Time it rings,
  From the dim, forgotten beginning of things;
And back of the Voice is the Word;
  And the formless void heard
And the face of the deep was stirred.
  And back of the Word is omnipotent Thought,
Omniscient Spirit, in power that wrought,
  Infinite, Triune Creator, who brought
Light from the darkness and Life from the clod;
  In the beginning, God.

The Creator

HE takes the scent of the softening ground
    Where the first green blade pricks through
    He takes the reddening maple bough
  A-slant against the blue,
He takes the cheer in the robin's song
  And the flash of the blue-bird's wing,
The joy of prisoned things set free,—
  And of these he makes the Spring.

He takes the sheen of the waving wheat
  Where the slow cloud-shadows pass,
He takes the brook's soft rippling tune
  And the daisied meadow grass,
He takes the swish of the mower's scythe
  In the noontide's hot, white glare,
The joy of labor and growing things,—
  And makes the Summer fair.

He takes the sound of the dropping nuts
    And the scent of the wine-sweet air
In the twilight time of the year's long day,
    When the spent Earth kneels in prayer,
He takes a thousand varied hues
    Aglow in an opal haze,
The joy of the harvests gathered in,—
    And makes the Autumn days.

He takes the peace of the snowy fields,
    Asleep 'neath the clear, cold moon,
He takes the grace of the leafless trees
    That sway to the wind's wild rune,
The frost-made lace on the window pane,
    The whirl of the starry flakes,
The joy of the rest when toil is done,—
    And the quiet Winter makes.

He takes the years,—the old, the new,
    With their changing scenes and brief,
The close-shut bud and the fruiting bough,
    Flower and fading leaf,
Grace and glory and lack and loss,
    The song, the sigh, the strife,
The joy of hope and the hope fulfilled,—
    And makes of the years a life.

He takes our lives and the sum of them,
    His will and the will of man,
Evil and good and dream and deed,
    His purpose and our plan,
The thwarted lives and the crippled lives
    And the things that give them worth,
The joy of life and the pain of life,—
    And makes the Heavens and Earth.

The Making of the Beautiful

MEADOW and vale and mountain,
  Ocean and lake and wood,—
God looked on the fruit of His labor
And saw that His work was good;
And yet was there something lacking
  In the world that he had made,
Something to brighten the greenness,
  Something to lighten the shade?

He took a shred of the rainbow,
  A bit of the sunshine's gold,
The colors of all the jewels
  The mines of earth enfold,
A piece of the mist of evening
  With the sunset woven through,
A scrap of the sky at noonday,
  A clear, unclouded blue.

Of these He fashioned the flowers,
  And some were red, like the rose,
And some were a lovely azure,
  And some were pale as the snows;
Some, shaped like a fairy chalice
  The perfumed honey to hold,
And some were stars of silver,
  And some were flakes of gold.

They flashed in the gloom of the forests,
  They clung to the boughs of the trees,
They hid in the grass of the meadows,
  They drifted away on the breeze,
They fell in the clefts of the canyons
  And high on the mountains bare,
Where never an eye should see them
  Save His Who had made them fair.
        *   *   *   *   *   *   *   *   *

But still there was something wanting,
  His labor was not yet done;

He gathered more of the colors
  Of rainbow and sky and sun,
And now unto these He added
  The music of sea and land,
The tune of the rippling river,
  The splash of the waves on the sand,
The raindrops' lilting measure,
  The pine tree's crooning sigh,
The aspen's lisping murmur,
  The wind's low lullaby,
Faint fluting of angel voices
  From heavenly courts afar,
And the softest, dreamiest echoes
  Of the song of the morning star.

Then deftly His fingers moulded
  The strong and the delicate things
Instinct with the joy and the beauty
  Of song and of soaring wings;
Nightingale, heron and seagull,
  Bobolink, lark—and then,
I think that He smiled a little
  As He tilted the tail of the wren,
As He made the owl's face solemn
  And twisted the blue jay's crest,
As He bent the beak of the parrot
  And smoothed the oriole's vest,
As He burnished the crow's jet plumage
  And the robin's breast of red;
"In the cold of the northern springtime
  The children will love it," He said.
So some were quaint and cunning,
  And some were only fair,
And some He gave a song to,
  And lo, the birds of the air.

And the snippets of things left over,
  He tossed out under the skies,
Where, falling, fluttering, flying,
  Behold, they were butterflies!

Page Seven

Tom Thumb Yellowbird

GLINT of sunshine and a song;
This is Tom Thumb Yellowbird;
Sure, from such a tiny mite
Louder strain was never heard.

Just a pair of wings and throat,
Midget chorister of glee;
Just two sunbeams and a voice,
Sublimated melody.

True sun-worshipper is he,
Devotee of summertime;
Naught of frost or blight he knows,
Following warmth from clime to clime

Steeped in sunlight through and through,
Feathered morsel of pure gold,
Greatheart atom, brimming o'er
With the joy he cannot hold.

Gleam of sun, by shadow chased,
Flitting in and out the trees;
Thumb-nail sketch of energy,
Busy as the murmuring bees.

Soul of glad contentment he,
Happy, happy all the day,
Sweetening toil from dawn to dusk
With his tireless roundelay.

The Phoebe Bird

WHEN springtime days are bright and fair
  And skies are blue and shining,
  A lonely little bachelor
Goes grieving and repining;
Among the budding orchard trees
 From dawn to dark he's calling,
Athwart the robins' cheery tones
 His plaintive accents falling—
  "Phœ-be—Phœ-be—where's Phœ-be?"

O cruel must the maiden be
 To leave him thus despairing,
The while she loiters on the road
 For his distress uncaring!
When other birds are glad and gay
 And blithely they are singing,
He still repeats his pleading cry
 As here and there he's winging—
  "Phœ-be—Phœ-be—come, Phœ-be!"

He has no heart his home to plan—
 That nest of dainty beauty—
Till she has come his toil to share
 In wifely love and duty.
So all the day this faithful swain
 His loneliness is voicing;
O Phœbe, come, and end his plaint,
 And he shall sing, rejoicing,
  "Phœ-be—Phœ-be—here's Phœ-be!"

The Little Birds of God

I HEAR them at my window in the late, gray
winter dawn,
The little birds of God, the farthing sparrows
of His care;
They ask of me, as I of Him, His gift of daily bread.
With soft, impatient twitterings they voice their
morning prayer.

The heavenly Father feedeth them, the little birds
of God,
Though 'tis my hand that scattereth the food
within their reach;
I do but share His bounty when I give the crumbs
to them.
O doubting heart and anxious heart, what lessons
they can teach!

They sow not, neither do they reap, nor gather into
barns,
Content if but each day shall bring the day's
supply of food;
No question whence it comes, nor if the morrow
bringeth more—
Small optimists in feathers, who are sure that all
is good!

God seeth when they fly or fall. Am I less worth
than they?
I would not fail them in their need. Is He less
true than I?
I would not mock their faith in me, nor hurt them,
nor betray;
I answer to their trusting call, He to His children's
cry.

When sunset tints the fading light and dusk is
  falling fast,
  The while I draw the curtains close and stir the
    hearth-fire bright,
I hear their cheerful chirping, the little birds of God,
  And wonder to what shelter they are fleeing for
    the night.

But they, as I, shall rest secure beneath the wings
  of Love,
  Though storm and darkness sweep the sea and
    cover all the land.
My life and theirs, so small and frail, God's care of
  both the same;
  My soul a nesting bird within the hollow of His
    hand.

In February

OH, they say it's growing colder every day,
  That the winter's growing bolder every day
  Since the bear's gone back to sleep
In his cavern dark and deep,
There'll be six weeks more of snowing,
Of freezing and of blowing—every day.

But the day's a little longer every day,
And the sun's a little stronger every day;
If we're patient for a while,
We shall see the summer smile,
And the buds will soon be showing,
For they're growing, growing, growing every day

And the birds will soon be singing every day,
Northward now they'll soon be winging every day;
Though the frost is in the air,
There's a feeling everywhere
That the skies are growing clearer,
And the springtime's drawing nearer every day.

When the Leaves Fall

WHEN sunny days and frosty nights
　　Have wrought their mystic alchemies,
　　With amber warp and woof of flame
They weave their Orient tapestries;
And where the leafy tents of green
　　All summer long their shadows cast,
October's gay pavilions stand
　　Till levelled by November's blast.

Green leaves and golden—fair were they;
　　But beautiful, when they are gone,
The changing pageant of the skies,
　　The drifting clouds, the rose of dawn;
And, when those splendid curtains fall
　　That nightly foiled the peeping stars,
I note the blaze of sunset fires
　　And catch the ruby glow of Mars;

I see pale Venus' lamp of pearl
　　Across the purpling heavens' arch
Flash signal to the hosts of night
　　To recommence their stately march,
And watch while world on radiant world
　　With answering gleam wheels into place,
Until the fiery dot-and-dash,
　　Far-glimmering, fills the deeps of space,

So doth the near obscure the far,
　　The earthly hide the heavenly view,
And life must oft some glory lose
　　Ere we can see the stars shine through.

When Sir Oriole Comes

WHEN the oriole has come,
　　Then I know that summer's here;
　　He's no Spartan, to endure
Frost-nipped toes with smiling cheer.
Long ago the waiting Spring
　　Sent her mystic summons forth,
And in haste, with clanging cries,
　　Rose the wild geese, faring north.
Robin came when March winds keen
　　Ruffled all his feathers bright,
And the flickers' harsh "Ha! Ha!"
　　Mocked old Winter's tardy flight.
Bluebird followed, goldfinch too,
　　Then the summer yellowbird,
Acolyte at Summer's shrine;
　　All day long his chant was heard.

So at last the stage was set
　　For the court of Queen of May;
Prince of all her cavaliers,
　　Came Sir Oriole, blithe and gay.
Watch him preen his scarlet coat
　　In the blossoming cherry-tree,
Breathing in the fragrance soft;
　　O, a sybarite is he!
Does he know—the dainty elf—
　　How he glorifies the scene,
Like a flaming jewel set
　　In the white and pearly green?
Did he choose the place with care?
　　Little bunch of vanity!
Crooning, plaintive, all the while,
　　Such a wooing melody,

Such a tender, witching call
　For his loitering mate to come,
Slim and sleek in satin gown,
　Quaker beauty, shyly dumb.
Now, a blazing shaft of light,
　See him flash athwart the bloom!
O, I know the summer's here,
　For the oriole has come.

The Bird's Message

SING, little birds, oh, sing!
　　You come while the trees are bare,
　While frost yet locks the streams
And the north wind chills the air;
You trust that the green leaves wait,
　Sunshine, and summer's breath;
Oh, teach us your simple faith
　That life shall follow death.

Sing, little birds, oh, sing!
　Give us the message of God,
That under the cloudy skies
　And up from the frozen sod
The seeds that we sow shall spring
　To life and beauty and bloom,
And that so shall our dead arise
　From the dark and silent tomb.

Sing, little birds, oh, sing!
　Our hearts are heavy with grief,
And under the darkened skies
　We doubt of flower and leaf,
Doubt that the earth yet lives,
　Cold in its shroud of snow;
Sing, little birds, oh, sing!
　We doubt, but you know—you know.

The Bridge Builders

OH, never the land of their birth can hold them!
   The wastes untrodden shall call them far,
   Where winds of an alien clime enfold them,
Lone 'neath the light of a stranger star.
Earth makes them free of her secret places,
   And one with her ageless solitudes;
The heirs are they of her high, still spaces,
   Friends of the forest, and wards of the woods

Their foes are the swamp, the racing river,
   Fathomless quicksand and jungle's breath,
The icy chill and the wasting fever,
   Imminent danger and waiting death;
But theirs the courage to face disaster,
   The stubborn patience, the cunning skill;
The forces of nature they meet and master,
   Tame and bend to their utmost will.

Where the hush of creation rests unbroken
   Their shrieking whistles that calm shall break;
Where never the voice of man hath spoken
   Their drills and hammers the echoes wake.
At their commandment the rocks are riven,
   The mountains move and the seas are stayed,
Where wild beasts hunted their stakes are driven,
   Where eagles nested their trail is made.

With chain and compass and line and plummet
   They gauge and measure and bound their dream;
They pierce the peak and they scale the summit,
   Harness the torrent and halt the stream;
Where plunging cataracts fall in thunder
   Their airy webs o'er the void are hung;
Where whirlpools whiten, the girders under,
   Their piers are fixed and their trestles flung

They level the hill and they fill the hollow
   To make a road for the men who roam,
Smooth and straight for the feet that follow,
   Seeking for pleasure or gold or home.
Though hidden treasure their picks uncover,
   They leave and lose it and still press on;
In the van of progress their armies hover,
   Here today, and tomorrow gone.

Before them the silence of desolation,
   Waterless desert and treeless plain;
Behind them the tread of a marching nation,
   Roaring cities and leagues of grain.
The wilderness yields to their slow persistence,
   The reef and the tundra their word await;
The peaceful victors of space and distance,
   The mighty masters of time and fate!

The First Song-Sparrow

"OH, SPRING is coming!" trills the robin bold
   While still the wind is blowing bleak and
      cold,
And rags and tatters left by winter drear
In lingering fringes of the snow appear,
The cheery prophet of a good to be,
With no regard for what his eye may see
Hurls brave defiance at the stormy skies,
And sturdily repeats his prophecies.

But sudden comes a day of softer air
With still, warm sunshine lying everywhere;
The leafless trees a sharper shadow throw,
And vanished every vestige of the snow;
A silver haze blurs all the hard blue sky,
And veils the distant hills in mystery;
Then, gently, joyous, tender, and serene,
As if the promised good at last were seen,
I hear the first song-sparrow of the year
With confidence proclaiming, "Spring is *here*."

Spring Song of Praise

PRAISE the Lord, ye heavens of heavens,
  Sun and moon and stars of light;
  Praise Him, all His vast creation,
Deepest deep and highest height.
Praise Him, meadow, mount and valley,
  Praise Him, forest, field and stream,
Praise Him, sky and earth and ocean,
  Roused from winter's chilling dream.

Praise Him, all ye wild winds blowing,
  Sweeping cloudy heavens clear;
Praise Him, ye that reap your sowing,
  For the seed time of the year;
Praise Him, all ye leaf buds breaking
  From the naked bough's rent sheath;
Praise Him, all ye brown seeds waking
  In the dark, the sod beneath.

Praise Him, all ye green things growing
  Where the harvest yet shall be;
Praise Him, all ye waters flowing
  From your icy fetters free;
Praise Him, all ye blithe birds winging
  From afar your trackless flight;
Praise Him, butterflies upspringing
  From your torn shrouds to the light.

For the pledge of Life Immortal,
  Writ in sunshine, song and bloom;
For the lamp at Death's dark portal
  Lit within His empty Tomb;
For the Resurrection story
  By each spring-time told again;
For the vision and the glory;—
  Praise the Lord, ye sons of men!

The Butterfly

HE that kills a worm
  Kills a butterfly.
In the ugly form
Of the crawling thing
Folded lies the wing
That shall cleave the sky;
In the creeping worm
  Doomed his way to plod
With no thought nor care
  Higher than the sod,
Rests the spirit form
  Clothed in beauty rare,
That shall mount on high
  Free of earth and air;
Once this shape outgrown
  Comes the bliss of flight,
  Glory and delight
To the clod unknown.
Spare the slow, dull form,
  Pass the creature by,
He that kills a worm
  Kills a butterfly.

Does the sluggish thing,
  Waiting dull and dumb,
Feel the folded wing,
  Dream of joys to come?
Does he go his ways
Through the long, slow days,
Knowing that they tend
All to one sure end?

Worm, I thrill with thee!
  Eager and elate,
  Fettered here I wait
For the life to be;

Feel the folded wings
  Faintly stir and rise,
While the clay that clings
  Holds them from the skies.

Though the body wear
Old with fret and care,
Though it weary grow
  Of the treadmill round,
Plodding dull and slow
  Here upon the ground,—
Grant, O Lord of Life!
  That the wings of me,
  Struggling to be free,
May emerge from strife,
Sorrow, toil and pain
With no spot nor stain;
May unmarred escape
From this mortal shape.
May I ever strive
These to keep alive,
These from death to save
And the body's grave;
Patient may I bide,—
Though unsatisfied,
Still content to stay
My appointed day,
Till the shrouded soul,
Loosed from dark and dole,
From the clay that clings—
  Chrysalis that holds,
  Hampers and enfolds—
Spreads at last its wings,
  Evermore to be
One with life and Thee.

The Holly Tree

OH, make an emblem of the holly tree!
Its green recalls the palm of victory,
The martyr's sign of triumph in the strife,
The deathless hope in that immortal life
Which every Spring, rejoicing, typifies;
Its red is love and joy and sacrifice.
True type of fortitude and patient cheer,
It will not pine though all the world be drear;
The Winter wraps it in the snowdrifts chill—
It lifts its head with sturdy courage still,
Shakes from its boughs the clinging mass of white
And shows its coronal of berries bright
That hold the Summer in their hearts, and glow
Like living coals amid the ashes' snow,
The garnered sunshine of a life's long way,
The bits of brightness in the wintry day.

So leaf and berry each its story tells,
But there's another word the holly spells;
What links it, brave amid the wintry snows,
With the frail sweetness of the summer rose?
Yet both in bristling thorns are panoplied
And for their capture many a hand has bled.
What is the meaning here unless it be
That far more precious than the leafy tree
Or the fair beauty of the Summer's bloom—
Its airy grace and delicate perfume—
Are the sharp thorns that rouse from selfish peace,
From "primrose paths" and flowery ways of ease,
And prick us from a life of low content
To spur us onward to the mount's ascent?

From weakness strength shall come, from bitter,
    sweet,
And bloom and berry thus be made complete;
For strength and sweetness must perfected be
By pain—the thorns of rose and holly tree.

No kinglier crown man's brows have ever worn
Than that one fashioned from the platted thorn,
And sometimes unto us a thorn is lent
Until we make the pain a sacrament.
For no man knows the best that life can give
Until by dying he has learned to live;
Until the crown of suffering he has worn,
And known the compensation of the thorn.

Morning Glories

LITTLE bits of bloom celestial
   On the earth reborn,
   Pink and purple, snow and azure,
Each new day adorn;
Little chalices of beauty,
   Trumpets of delight,
Cups of joy distilled in darkness
   From the dews of night.
Fragile beauty, fleeting glory,
   Short the hour that's given;
Yet each night and morning finds them
   So much nearer heaven;
Though the blossoms droop and wither,
   Still the clinging vine
Round each bar that lifts it higher
   Eagerly will twine;
Striving, reaching, grasping, holding,
   Upward, o'er and o'er,
So the heavenly morning-glories
   Seek their home once more.

Let our hearts thus greet each morning,
   Joyous as the day;
Let our souls thus climb to heaven
   From the earth away.

The Sea Shell

HERE let it lie, beside its ancient home,
  Nor bear it far away from all it knows,
  From all it loves, remembers and desires;
Fit toy for Aphrodite, ere she rose.

From cradle-rockings of the summer seas
  To be the joy and solace of the earth.
So leave it here; the tide may draw it back
  To those translucent depths that gave it birth.

What music murmurous yet fills its heart,—
  What haunting fragments of lost melodies,
What lovely half-forgotten minor strains,
  What crashing chords and stormy symphonies;

What rippling lullabies in still lagoons,
  What flooding harmonies of winds and waves,
What mournful requiems on coral reefs,
  What organ anthems o'er unquiet graves.

Could we but know what memories it keeps!
  Perchance upon a far-off, golden morn
It saw the sportive Nereids at play,
  And heard some Triton blow his wreathed horn

Perchance it heard the clash of smitten shields
  Half drown the thunder shout of Cyrus' horde,—
"Thalassa!" and "Thalassa!" ringing down
  The slope o'er which the great Ten Thousand
  poured.

Perchance it saw the Argonaut's brave prows
  Turn seaward on their argent questing long;
Perchance it watched Ulysses at the mast,
  Self-bound, drift past the sirens' luring song;

Perchance it heard the wrathful tempest roar
   That whelmed Leander in its seething tide,
And saw the flickering torchlight paint the wave
   That beat against the rocks where Hero died.

So, leave it here upon the wave-wet sand,
   Among the seaweed and the flying foam,
That soon the ebbing tide may draw it back
   And bear it downward to its ancient home.

The Camp Fire

CHEERILY crackles the morning fire,
    While the red flashes mount higher and
      higher;
Twisting and bending, smoke wreaths ascending,
Earth sounds and air sounds in harmony blending;
Bright through the tree tops the sunlight is falling,
Joy is awaking! A new day is breaking!
Rise to its labors, your slumbers forsaking;
Heap on the fagots, stir the blaze higher,—
Cheerily, cosily, crackles the fire.
        Good morning!

Dreamily flickers the evening fire
While the dusk shadows creep higher and higher,
Daylight is ending, quiet's descending,
Earth sounds and air sounds in peacefulness
    blending;
Dim through the tree tops the starlight is falling,
 Soft in the silence a drowsy bird's calling;
Sleepily winking, stealthily blinking,
All the red coals into ashes are sinking.
Cover the embers lest it burn higher,—
Dreamily, drowsily smoulders the fire.
        Good night!

The Water-Lily's Story

WHEN first I woke to life,
   Deep down in the river's bed,
   I could not breathe for the stifling ooze
And the blackness over my head.
In darkness I longed for the light,
   Prisoned, I yearned to be free,
In dreams I pined for the sky and the wind,
   For star and bird and tree;
And I said: "I will rise to that upper air,
   And the life that draweth me."

The twining weeds of the water-world
   Reached out and held me fast;
The lithe reeds wove a tangled net
   To catch me as I passed;
The creeping things of mire and mud
   Beckoned and bade me stay;
In the treacherous current, swift and strong,
   I felt my weak stem sway;
But through them, over them, past them all,
   I took my upward way.

Till, white, white,
   Brimmed with sunshine and steeped in light,
I lifted up my fragrant cup—
   Bloom of the daytime and star of the night—
In rapture I gazed at the heavens blue
   And knew that all my dreams were true.
And pure and fair my white leaves bear
   Never a trace of slime and mold,
And the crawling things of the under-world
   Have left no taint on my heart of gold.
In peace I rest on the river's breast,
   And living, I love, and, loving, live,
And, breathing deep of that upper air,
   My life to the world in sweetness give.

In the stifling air of the lower world,
Oh, Soul, do you dream, as I,
Of the pure, clear light and the sunshine's gold,
And the blue of the open sky?
Rise from your dreaming and lift your head
From the death-in-life of the clinging clay,
And, spurning every base desire,
Mounting higher and yet higher,
Hold on your upward way

Till, pure and white,
Filled with glory and steeped in light,
No trace of the soil from whence it springs
Staining the Soul's expanding wings,
You too
Shall see the arching heaven's blue
And find that all your dreams are true.
You shall eat of joy as your daily bread,
Through love you shall learn and by loving live;
You shall drink of life at the fountain head,
And that life to the world in sweetness give.

This is the Day

*This is the day that the Lord hath made. I will rejoice
and be glad in it. Psalm.*

SIGH of the breezes or sob of the tempest,
Skies of pure azure or clouds hanging low,
Sunshine or frost or the lash of the storm
wind,
Veiling of mist or the white whirl of snow;
Welcome the day! for the Lord, He hath made it,
Cometh it golden or cometh it gray.
Bringeth it burden or giveth it guerdon,
Let us rejoice and be glad in His day.

The Song of Creation

THE sun and the cloud declare God's glory,
   The sea and the land repeat the story;
   From deep unto deep one theme is pealing,
From height unto height the echo stealing;
The day to the day one tale is telling,
And night unto night one word is spelling;
The voice of the wind in the desert crying
Is one with the croon of the pines replying;
The lilt in the note of the wild bird ringing
Is tuned to the choral the stars are singing;
One chant have lake and fount and river—
   Praise ye the Lord
   And bless His name forever.

One gladness the green of the grass is showing
And bright in the daffodil's gold is glowing;
One joy in the scent of the rose is breathing
And in the grace of the vine-leaves wreathing;
One rapture is felt by the sap upwelling
And by the veins of the leaf-bud swelling;
One bliss thro' the butterfly's wings is thrilling
And out of the crocus cup is spilling;
One hymn hath the heart of the earth a·quiver—
   Praise ye the Lord
   And bless His name forever.

From generation to generation
   The heavens and earth with His praises ring,
And lo! the pæan of all creation
   Is one with the anthem the angels sing;
The saints have learned it with tears and crying
   In earthly sorrow and earthly night,
The lips of the ransomed, unvexed by sighing,
   Shall breathe it with rapture in cloudless light,
And the surging tide of their jubilation
   Through years eternal shall still be rolled
By every people and tribe and nation
   In that new song that is yet the old;

And sweet shall it sound by the crystal river—
    Praise ye the Lord
    And bless His name forever.

All else may fail, His goodness faileth never,
All else may change, His love is changeless ever,
From age to age, forever more the same—
Praise ye the Lord and magnify His name.

Apple Blossoms

GOD might have clothed the apple-trees
    In scentless brown or gray—
    Such frail and fleeting blossoming,
So soon to pass away—

Instead of this fair springtime garb
    Of fragrant pink and pearl
That flutters down like rosy snow
    On every breeze a-whirl.

His goodness gives the pleasant fruit
    On laden boughs down-bent;
His loving-kindness adds the bloom,
    Its beauty and its scent.

He loads us with His benefits
    Until no want we know,
And then He sends the little more
    That makes our cup o'erflow.

He opens wide His hand of love;
    He gives no stingy dole;
His tender mercies crown our days;—
    O bless the Lord, my soul!

The Lullaby of Rain

THROUGH the sultry city daylight I had toiled
    with throbbing head,
    But at night, though spent and weary, slum-
ber from my wooing fled;
Still before my aching vision lines of figures came
    and went,
Ghosts of those long hours of labor and the day's
    imprisonment.
Only glare and tumult entered through the window
    opened wide,
Naught of freshness e'er could reach me from the
    surging human tide;
Then a muttered growl of thunder and the light-
    ning's far-off flare,
And a sudden breath of coolness in the hot and
    murky air;
There's a patter on the shingles and a tap against
    the pane,—
Oh, the orchestra is tuning for the Lullaby of Rain!

Now the spell it weaves about me wraps me in its
    mesh of dreams
Till reality is blended with the thing that only seems,
And my sigh of soft contentment wafts my thought,
    like homing dove,
Straight, on swift unerring pinion to a little house
    I love.
Far away from city pavements, never jangling sound
    it hears,
Watcher of the dawns and sunsets through the
    peaceful passing years;
When the twilight calm enfolds it and the purple
    mists arise,   (eyes!
Oh, that still, unlighted darkness is a rest for tired
Like a whispered benediction falls the hush of even-
    tide,
Changeless through the changing seasons doth my
    House of Memories bide.

* * * * * * * * *

I can hear the water running from the overhanging
    eaves.
And a liquid, lisping trickle from the elm-tree's
    drooping leaves,
There's a clatter on the shingles and a splash against
    the pane,—
Oh, I know the blessed prelude to the Lullaby of
    Rain.
Sweeter than the censer's fragrance is the orchard's
    rosy bloom,
Spicy odors floating upward to that low-ceiled attic
    room;
Dim against the outer blackness gleams the win-
    dow's open space,
And the faint, elusive earth-scents, drifting through
    it, cool my face.
I can smell the fresh wet lilacs from the bush beside
    the door,
And the quick tears burn my eyelids—I shall enter
    there no more.
I can hear the sleepy twitter of a bird's note from
    the trees,
And the meadow-brook's hoarse murmur, borne
    upon the rising breeze;
There's a choked and chuckling gurgle from the
    overflowing eaves,
And a drip! drip! drip! *staccato* from the soaked
    and streaming leaves,
Then a rush along the shingles and a dash against
    the pane,—
Oh, a hundred voices mingle in the Lullaby of Rain!
Now the single sounds are merging in a long.
    crescendo roar
That shall drown all lesser noises in its steady
    pelting pour;
Hence, ye phantoms of old labor! ye shall haunt me
    now in vain
As I drift away to dreamland to the Lullaby of Rain.

In the Winter Woods

IN the desolate forest the snow-wreaths cover
The dead things over with ermine pall,
And the bare brown cup of a nest forsaken,
Where no birds waken with jocund call,
Is filled with the silence of cold flakes drifting
And lightly sifting, that o'er it fall.

But neither of grief nor of gloom 'tis telling,
This empty dwelling where song is stilled;
It whispers yet of a day of gladness
Untouched by sadness, with joyance thrilled,
Of a dream come true, of a finished story,
The rainbow glory of Hope fulfilled.

'Twas a cup poured full of the wine of pleasure,
Unstinted measure o'erflowed its brim,
And the near, and the far, and the new, the olden,
The gray, the golden, to Earth's wide rim,
Had each a share in that joy of living,
A beauty giving no cloud might dim.

For your hearts were in tune with the great Earth
Mother's,
O Little Brothers of Airy Flight!
No fear of the future your thoughts invading,
Of green leaves fading or skies less bright;
Since you knew, ere the chill of the frost could
scare you,
Your wings would bear you beyond its blight.

O wee, brave souls of a cheer unfailing!
How unavailing the loads we bear;
And oft I long, when I hear you singing,
Your far flight winging through sunlit air,
To rise, like you, to the Heavenly places,
In wide, free spaces to lose my care.

But our thoughts may mount as you rise, and follow
  Like homing swallow that seeks her mate,
As you lead them up through the low clouds trailing,
  Its glory veiling, to Heaven's gate,
From the Land of the Perfect Peace to borrow
  The balm of sorrow, for which we wait.

Dear earth-born dwellers, akin to Heaven,
  To you is given a mission sweet;
Between them ever a chain you're weaving,
  The blue depths cleaving on pinions fleet,
And the notes you glean at that radiant portal,
  From songs immortal, your own repeat.

In the hush of the woods, by their memories haunted
  A land enchanted, where dreams have birth,
I linger long, for I fain would capture
  The wraith of rapture, the ghost of mirth;
Yet I know they are shut in their snowy prison,
  Till Life, new-risen, shall wake the earth.

Forget-Me-Nots

WHEN Eve passed out of Eden,
    Beside its guarded gates
    She saw a flower blooming,
  Afar from all its mates;
And tearfully she raised it
  And tenderly she bore
Away from that loved garden
  Where she should walk no more

But grew the flower and flourished
  And lifted up its face
Bright with the Eden beauty,
  Fair with the Eden grace,
Dear blossom of remembrance,
  Blue as its native skies,
"Forget me not," still breathing
  For that lost Paradise.

The Flight of the Air-Ship

AHOY! Yacht Butterfly, loosing your moorings
   Whither, whither, away?
   Clearing the tops of the wind-tossed clover,
Where do you cruise today?

'Ware the web of the yellow spider
   Lurking beside the stream!
There by the cat-tails something's moving,
   Flickering flash and gleam;
Quick! up sail and away, O Captain!
   This is a craft to fear,—
Armored cruiser and merciless pirate,
      Dragonfly buccaneer!

Signal in passing the heavily-laden,
   Lumbering freighter-bees,
Riding at anchor or taking cargo,
   Moored in the apple-trees;
Steer you now for the upper currents,
   Northerly with them swing;
Here go the clipper-built ships of the Air-Line,
   Birds of the tireless wing.

Far beneath you, in shine and shimmer
   Map of the world's unrolled;
Burnished buttercups glow and glisten,
   Field of the Cloth of Gold,
Riotous breezes are blowing the blossoms,
   Wheat-heads ripple and bow,
Foam-like the green of the poplars whitens
   Under your dancing prow.

Oh! the day is a dream of beauty,
   Long are the hours and bright,
Slowly, slowly its radiance softens,
   Dims and darkens to night;

Swallows, tracing their curves of beauty,
  Circle the sapphire dome;
Turn you, turn you, O Butterfly Skipper!
  Tack for the Port of Home.

Hoarse and plaintive the whippoorwill's crying
  Rings from the wooded crest,
Hark to the call of the bo'sun Robin,
  Piping the world to rest;
Faintly fragrant the primrose opens,
  Fire-flies winking nigh;
Droning beetles plow clumsily homeward,
  Humming-bird-moth scuds by.

Cool and dewy the shadows lengthen,
  Stretching across the vale,
A silver shallop, the new moon's floating
  Out where the West grows pale.
Where shall the fitful zephyrs bear you?
  Where does your harbor lie?
There where the masts of the pine-trees tower,
  Looming against the sky?

Nearer, nearer the slack tide drifts you,
  Voyage is almost past;
Furl your sails, O Butterfly Captain!
  Haven is reached at last.

The Moon

THE priestess of the Sun,
    At his deserted shrine
    Within the temple of the day
Where he has ceased to shine,
Where in the scented dusk
    The pale star-tapers burn,—
Re-lights the smouldering altar fire
And waits her lord's return.

Page Thirty-three

The Crag of the Cross

(A Natural Formation on the Island of Manan, in the Bay of Fundy.)

BESIDE the bleak coast of the Northland,
where winds with the tempests keep tryst,
Amid a wild welter of waters, an island looms
out of the mist;
Forever the high tides of Fundy sweep past with a
rush and a roar,
Forever the gulls cry their warning when fog
wreathes the desolate shore;
Above the gray billows the cliffs frown, above the
grim cliffs bends the sky,
And clear against cliff-side and heavens the Crag
of the Cross rises high.

Of old hath He laid its foundations who holdeth the
sea in His hand,
Who weigheth its waters by measure and setteth
their bounds by the sand;
And slowly His craftsmen have carved it,—the frost
and the storm and the wave—
Rough-hewn from the rock everlasting where æons
their annals might grave.
Long, long ere o'er Bethlehem's manger the Star
shed its radiant light,
And long ere on Calvary's summit the noonday was
shrouded in night;
While kingdoms and nations had risen and played
their brief parts for a day,
And countless new creeds and old systems had
flourished and passed to decay;
While oracles lapsed into silence and prophets grew
weary and dumb,
The Cross, through the centuries waiting, was
pledge of a faith yet to come.

And never the surf overwhelms it and never the
surges o'erflow

Though still through the storm and the sunshine
    the treacherous tides come and go;
They toss, but they may not pass over; they roar,
    but they shall not prevail,
And day after day they are baffled and night after
    night they shall fail;
For ever in vain is their striving to foil the decree
    He hath made:—
"Thus far shalt thou come but no farther, and here
    shall thy proud waves be stayed,"
Their force and their arts all defying, the Crag
    every onset shall breast,
And come they in peace or in anger, at the foot of
    the cross they must rest.

In summer, like shimmering opals, the dawn-tinted
    waters will sleep
Till comes the mysterious signal and stealthily land-
    ward they creep;
With soft sighing whispers beguiling they playfully
    break on the beach,
With musical rippling and plashing the sweet sing-
    ing voices beseech.
Like sycophants fawning and coaxing, caressing and
    dimpling in glee;—
But ever the Cross rises silent, majestic, unmoved
    by their plea.

And winter's black hordes charge as vainly, hurled
    forward with thunderous shocks,
With crash of relentless battalions and rending and
    grinding of rocks;
Urged on by the lash of the storm-wind and heedless
    of all in their path,
They batter the outlying ridges with hissing white
    torrents of wrath,
Till, raging in impotent fury, before the great Crag
    they retreat,
And, beaten to sullen submission, come crouching
    again at its feet.

Then, while the last sob of the tempest swells faint
    from the darkening west,
In billows all jade in the hollow and burnished to
    gold on the crest,
Up out of the seas of the Tropics the moon leads
    her glittering host—
The ranks of her silver-clad cohorts—to fling them
    once more on the coast.
The half-sunken ledges are covered, the shallows
    are flooded and filled,
Afar in the echoing caverns the deep organ-murmurs
    are stilled;
Above the heaped rocks of the shore-line the foam-
    whitened breakers shall toss,
Till over the wide waste of waters there rises naught
    else but the Cross.
So sink man's achievements and triumphs beneath
    the gray flood of the years,
So vanish the works of his wisdom, the schools and
    the temples he rears,
So cease both his dream and his doing, so perish his
    purpose and thought,
So pass all his pride and his power and all that his
    power hath wrought;
His tombs and his towers are shattered and buried
    in slow-drifting sand,
His columns of victory fallen, laid low by Time's
    leveling hand,
His cities are dust-heaps and ruins in deserts
    untrodden and lone,
Their splendor long lost and forgotten, their names
    and their places unknown
He writes on a shore that already is wet with the
    oncoming spray,
Where swift-flowing tides shall efface it and blot
    out his records for aye;
He spendeth his life as a shadow and only its
    passing is sure;—
But through all the ages unchanging, the Cross and
    its glory endure.

The Robin's Note

BLITHE bird of the morning, that heralds the
dawn,
How joyous the sound of his carolling free;
Ere the first gleam of silver has brightened the east
  He sings that the night and the darkness shall flee,
And a memory sweet and a prophecy sure
  Are mingled in one in that jubilant strain—
Grief and gladness long past, grief and gladness to
    come—
  Till my heart swells in answer with joy and with
    pain.
"Be cheery, my dearie, day's coming, night's gone;
Far up in the treetop I welcome the dawn.
There's a nestful of love and all heaven above,
No clouds in the blue but the sun can shine through.
So I sing all the day under bright skies or gray;
There's naught to be sad for and much to be glad for;
Be cheery, my dearie, keep singing alway."

Dear singer of sunset, I hear him at eve,
  When still is the blackbird and silent the thrush;
For a bliss bubbles over within his full heart
  Not even the coming of twilight can hush.
He sings in the sunshine and sings in the rain
  With a faith in the future no stormcloud can dim;
"In all things give thanks,"—he obeys the command,
  For shadow and sun seem alike unto him.
"Be cheery, my dearie, look up and be glad;
Though the weather be dreary, oh, never be sad!
Let it rain if it will; though the wind may be chill,
Over gray skies are blue, and the sun will shine
    through.
So I sing just as clear when the day's dark and
    drear;
There's much to be glad for and naught to be sad for;
Be cheery, my dearie, keep singing alway."

The Song of Running Water

THE song of running water: adown the mountain side
The brown brook hurries to its tryst like bridegroom to his bride;
It tinkles through the frosty night and babbles all the day,
And foams in wild impatience at each hindrance by the way,
Till at the wood's dusk entrance it checks its arrowy rush
To list the sighing of the pines, the vespers of the thrush;
It glides between its mossy banks in ripples sweet and cool,
Or pauses for the trout to leap in shadowy, rock-girt pool;
Then, "Follow—follow—follow!" it calls with laughing lure,
It sings the song of liberty, untrammeled, joyous pure.

The song of running water: the meadow stream in tune
With all the sounds of summer and the golden lights of June;
It rests in clear, dark shallows beneath the dreaming trees,
Still mirror for the drifting fleets of heaven's argosies.
It purls in mimic eddies around the larger stones
And croons its lullaby of peace in lilting undertones;
"Oh, hush! Oh, hush!" it whispers to the trailing grasses green,
And shy forget-me-nots that o'er its lazy current lean.
Who would not loiter with it along its winding ways?
It sings the song of idleness and long, bright, happy days.

The song of running water: the river's chanted hymn
From canyon walls that soar aloft like vast cathedral
    dim;
And where its leaping cataracts fling high their
    rainbow spray,
Like some great organ's solemn tones its rolling
    thunders play.
The valleys robe themselves in beauty wheresoe'er
    it flows,
And in its path the wilderness shall blossom as the
    rose.
Beside it shall the hungry a dwelling place prepare,
And plant the vines and sow the fields and reap
    their fruitage fair,
Past cities filled with toilers and grimy factory slaves,
With rush of mighty waters, soft sweep of racing
    waves,
It turns the wheels of labor and bears the ships to
    sea,
And sings the song of industry, untiring, glad and
    free.

But brook, or stream, or river, whatever name it
    bears,
That song can soothe my restless moods and charm
    away my cares.
And oft when waking weariness would hold me far
    from sleep,
The memory of its melody has lulled to slumber deep.
Yet is its meaning all unknown, its thought a mystery
Though bird and wind and forest have each a word
    for me;
The fields are friendly comrades, the sky a beckon
    ing hand,
But oh! the murmuring water I cannot understand
I hush my heart to listen, I hear its haunting strain,
A voice from that lost Paradise we may not here
    regain.

I have not learned its language, I do not know its
    speech,
And dead to me the secrets of the wonders it would
    teach.
Nor shall I ever comprehend till, past all pain and
    strife,
I wake where from the throne of God springs out
    the stream of life.

When all Eternity is ours and measured Time is
    o'er,
And finite in the Infinite is merged for evermore,
We shall not need its symbols and they shall cease
    to be;
We read as it is written: "There shall be no more
    sea."
No storm-tossed breakers, white with foam, no
    deadly undertow,
No ever-restless waves in that fair land to which
    we go,
No shifting sands, no ebbing tide salt as our sorrow's
    tears,
No sunken rocks, no stranded ships through all the
    deathless years.

But still the river runneth, to greet me with its song,
The music immemorial that I have loved so long.
With sound of many waters the crystal flood shall
    flow
And I shall find, in that clear voice, all voices that
    I know.
There shall the clue be given that eludes me here on
    earth;
These murmurs, half-articulate, of longing, grief
    and mirth,
The strange, wild, baffling harmonies from meadow,
    mount and wood,
Are blended there and reconciled, made plain and
    understood.

The scattered notes, the semi-tones, the broken
  chords, half-heard,
The plaintive minor cadences by jarring discords
  blurred,
Shall prove but parts of one great whole, a wondrous
  symphony
That our dull ears can never hear this side Eternity;
But there attuned to Heaven's tones, our finer
  sense shall feel
What Eden's muted echoes are striving to reveal,
Complex and many-sided, with mingled meanings
  rife,
The Song of Running Water is but the Song of Life.

How to Tell a Comet

Astronomy Made Easy.

THOUGH you may not know a planet
    From the bird that's called a gannet,
    Nor distinguish Sagittarius from Mars;
Though the beasts in that strange zoo
May all look alike to you,
    And you lump the whole caboodle just as "stars;"
Though you cannot place the lion,
Nor correctly trace Orion,
    Nor discern the jewelled belt he proudly wears,
Nor the big and little hounds,
Through those happy hunting grounds,
    Nightly chasing up the big and little bears;
Though you cannot tell the Dippers
From your grandpa's old felt slippers,
    And to name the constellations you would fail,
There's one thing that you may know
And be very sure it's so,—
    You can always tell a comet by its tail.
Its airy, hairy, winking, blinking, flowing, glowing
    tail;
Its fiery, wiry, gleaming, streaming, flaring, glaring
    tail.

My Trees

THEY do not stand in forest glade
  With moss and fern about their feet,
  Instead, they cast their pleasant shade
As warders of a village street;
Not theirs the brooding silence deep
  From dawn till dusk, from dark to day,—
They hear the housewife's cheery calls,
  The shouts of children at their play.
But sun and rain are kind to them,
  Their leaves dance with the dancing breeze,
And through the changes of the years
  I watch and love my neighbor trees.

I thrill with them when spring returns
  To rouse them from their peaceful dreams
With some elusive message borne
  By softer airs or murmuring streams;
When through the slowly lengthening days,
  All heedless of the lingering cold,
The first impatient birds arrive
  With wind-blown feathers, blithe and bold;
They sing amid the reddening boughs
  And choose the sites for future homes,
Serenely sure, through snow or sleet
  Or pelting rain, that summer comes.

I joy with them in long, bright days
  When leafy depths with life o'erflow;
The squirrels race from tree to tree
  And chatter madly as they go;
Through sultry noons and stifling nights,
  From their cool shade the locust shrills
His oft repeated prophecies
  Of heat that blights and drought that kills;
On one long branch above my roof
  The hang-bird's cradle sways and swings,
And when the hungry fledglings wake,
  With raucous calls the morning rings;

Then, fluttering down from stair to stair,
  With many a slip and anxious cry,
All spotted breasts and stumpy tails,
  The baby robins learn to fly.

I rest with them when autumn frosts
  Have changed their sober green array
To gorgeous garments, bright as brief,
  That fade and fall from day to day,
Revealing, through a thinning veil,
  Mute memories of summer past,
The small forsaken homes of song,
  Frail playthings for the winter's blast;
And when the early darkness comes,
  The moonbeams weave, with elfin grace,
Across the looms of leafless twigs
  Their magic mesh of shadow-lace.

I hope with them 'neath wintry skies,
  Nor do I feel them sad or chill;
Austere but beautiful they stand
  And read to me a lesson still;
They patient bide the waiting-time
  Of glory gone and beauty lost,
Assured that not a leaf shall fall
  And not a bough by storm be tossed,
Save but as part of God's great plan
  For them and me and all the earth,
And that a richer, fuller life
  Shall follow on this seeming dearth

One tells me of the mountain slopes,
  And one of ocean's myriad moods,
And one of some fair mirror-lake
  Enshrined in woodland solitudes;
My feet may never wander far
  To seek such varied joys as these,
But pent, like them, in village street,
  I am content—I have my trees.

The Winter Birds

WHEN autumn's flaming torch has set
  The hills and vales alight,
  Then gather all the feathered clans
To take their southward flight.
The goldfinch from the thicket flees,
  The swallow from the eaves,
His bower in the lilac bush
  The slim gray catbird leaves.

From meadow grass, from forest tree,
  Go bobolink and thrush,
And over fields and streams and woods
  There falls a sudden hush.
From all their summer haunts and homes
  The Singing Tribes are gone;
Oh, blessings on the winter birds
  That bravely linger on!

The flicker shouts across the fields,
  The cheery chickadee
Hobnobs with all the sparrow folk,
  Those birds of low degree;
The nuthatch makes his daily round,
  And hammers on the bark,—
Head up, head down, all one to him,—
  With many a loud remark.
I grant they are not musical,
  They sing no tuneful lays,
But oh, they give a wondrous charm
  To dull and gloomy days.

They break the deathlike calm that broods
  Above the earth's white shroud,
They twitter in the leafless trees
  Beneath the rainy cloud;
They drift before the coming storm,
  Half hid in falling snow,
Like little ghosts of autumn leaves
  Wind-driven to and fro.

When come the slow, dark winter morns,
  I hear them at my door,
They chirp their thanks for scattered crumbs,
  And boldly beg for more.

I love the robin's matin hymn,
  The blackbird's whistle clear,
The vesper sparrow's dulcet call
  When night is drawing near,
The yellow-bird's persistent chant,
  The phoebe's plaintive song;
But dear, as well, the simple notes
  That cheer the winter long.
And bright the robin's breast of red
  On some bleak day in spring,
And gay the oriole's flaming coat,
  The bluebird's azure wing;
But fair to me the winter birds
  In somber brown and gray,
The little brave and sturdy souls
  Who do not go away.

Christmas Roses

COLD and frost and storm wind under a
    leaden sky,—
    Surely beneath it all tender things and fair
  and sweet must die;
But lo! at our feet from the ice-bound earth,
  flushing with rosy glow,
Spring up the Christmas roses, blossoming under the
  snow.

Pain and hardship and trial and the stricken heart's
  low moan—
Surely the spirit of man must fail and his soul be
  overthrown;
Nay, for courage and patience and sweetness endure
  and grow,
Blossoming into beauty, like the roses under the
  snow.

From Forest to Fender

LOG that burns to ashes gray
    In my fireplace to-day,
        Could you speak, what would you say
Of the years long passed away?
Had you tongue, would you be telling
Of your ancient greenwood dwelling;
Of your boughs' exultant swelling
When the swift sap, hurrying on,
Told of Winter's numbness gone?
How March winds, like trumpets blowing,
Stirred the larch plumes into growing,
Roused the chestnuts' snowy splendor
And the birch-tree tassels slender?
How the flowers, frail and tender,
Frightened at the stormy sound,
Stayed safe hidden under ground
Till, like fairy fingers strumming,
April's raindrops, lightly drumming,
Sounded the reveille gay
For the blossoms of the May:

   "Snowdrop,—Crocus,—Violet,—
    Are you wrapped in slumber yet?
    Wake up, Daisy, Earth is waiting,
    Bluebirds in the trees are mating:
    Listen, Windflower, shy and sweet,
    Breezes pass with flying feet,
    Beckoning, calling, blithe and gay,
    'Little comrade, come and play.'
    Dandelion, please come up—
    Meadow-sweet, and Buttercup,
    Bright as newly-minted money;
    Bees are calling for their honey;
    You must hurry, Spring is here
    And the ground looks bare and drear
    Till you show your cheery faces,
    Fill with light the gloomy places!"

Did you see, down at your feet,
Pink and white arbutus sweet?
Watch the ferns doff woolly hoods,
As the sun crept through the woods?
See Jack in his pulpit preaching
Lessons of the Spring-time's teaching?
When the birds came, did you know?
Did you bend your branches low,
Sheltering every downy brood,
Lending to the motherhood
In that tiny bunch of feathers
Your protection in all weathers?

Did you love the Summer-time,
When the year was in its prime?
When your rugged trunk was rife
With its myriad insect life;
Where the ants ran up and down,
And the caterpillar brown
Took his toilsome way and slow
From the barren ground below;
Where the butterflies were born
On some bright and sunny morn,
Leaving but an empty shell
Of their burial to tell?

Did you hear the brown brook's song
Sounding blithely all day long,
As it plunged from sunlit meadow
Into your green gloom and shadow—
Hushing its gay babble there
To a softer, drowsier air?
See the cardinal-flowers stand
On its banks, a gallant band,
Each with flaming torch in hand?
Listen to the squirrels' chatter
Over some important matter?
Spy the Bee—sad, gossip rover!—
Whisp'ring secrets to the clover?
Watch the light wind, running over,
Sway the grass, where, safely hid,

Cricket gay and katydid,
Elfin minstrels, mad with glee,
Filled the air with melody?
Did you sigh when Autumn came,
Setting sumacs all aflame,
Putting goldenrod in ranks
Marching down the road-side banks,
Opening starry aster faces
In the meadows' vacant spaces;
Launching all the silky down
From the milkweed's pods of brown
On the currents of the breeze,
Sails all set for unknown seas?

And then, do you still remember
How your leaves fell in November?
And what story you were tracing
In the crossing and embracing,
Warp and woof and interlacing
Of the tiny twigs on high,
Outlined on the sapphire sky,
Etched upon the falling snow,—
White above and black below—
Or at sunset, dark and bold,
Set against the flame and gold
Like a spectral ship whose sails
Long since vanished in the gales,
Leaving masts and cordage bare?

This the lesson written there—
So I fancy—in the air:
    "Every day and every hour,
    Ripening berry, opening flower,
    Adds some beauty, gives some glory,
    Spells some new word in the story
    Nature ever is inditing
    For the eyes that read her writing.
    Leaves are fall'n, but branches left
    Cannot be of charm bereft;
    Grace of form, when color's gone,

Has a fairness all its own,
Like a heart that does its duty
Cheerful still, though robbed of beauty;
And, although of joy bereft,
Makes the best of what is left."

Oh, how could you help but love it—
Life and every aspect of it!
Rooted fast and yet so free,
Every leaf a thing of glee,
With God's heaven arched above you
And the forest things to love you.
Did they part you from your brothers
When they took you from the others?
Do you ever envy those
Standing yet amid the snows
While we light your funeral pyre,—
Dream and doze beside the fire?

Log that burns to ashes gray,
Could you speak, this would you say
Of the years long passed away:
"Winter's cold and Summer's heat
Made me strong and kept me sweet;
Summer's sun and Winter's snow—
Rest and action—helped me grow.
Like me, you must learn to bear
All that comes of dark or fair
Without murm'ring or repining,
Storing, when the sun is shining,
Light and heat for day's declining.
Flowers all withered, fruit all borne,
All your beauty from you torn,
So you too must fall at last—
Bent and broken in the blast—
By the axe of Time, the Trier.
Nay, what matter though you're old,
If you keep some heart from cold
By your fire!"

Nature's Shut-Ins

FERNS are the "shut-ins" of God's flower
   kingdom,
      Hidden in mossy dells and cool retreats;
Their lace-like fronds uncurl in fresh, green beauty
   Far from the busy world and dusty streets.

They bear no gorgeous flowers of gold or crimson,
   No dainty blooms of blue or pearly white;
Their graceful leaves exhale no strong, sweet odor,
   Their very seeds are hidden from our sight.

And yet, sometimes, to eyes that tire of brightness,
   To senses sated with a rich perfume,
How grateful is the cool green of the fern-leaves
   Set in the silence of some shaded room.

Can we not learn from them some blessed lesson,
   We, who, like them, are growing in the shade?
Their lovely freshness is a constant beauty,
   Dewy and sweet when summer blossoms fade.

When others come, who, dwelling in the sunshine,
   Have grown a-weary of the toil and strife,
Can we not share with them our calm and quiet—
   Show them the beauty of a hidden life?

May we not give to them some tender message,
   Some of the garnered peace we hold in store,
Some of the songs He giveth in the midnight,
   When sleep flies from us and the pain is sore?

They walk with hurrying steps Life's busy highway,
   Often the still, small voice they cannot hear;
But we can listen in the restful stillness
   Its words of faith and hope and gladsome cheer.

We dwell in safety in our Lord's green pastures,
   Our souls at rest the quiet waters by;
Willing to *be* since we may not be *doing*,
   Living epistles, open to the eye.

Our frail lives hidden in His strength eternal,
  Guarded and shielded from the tempest's shock,
The wild winds pass us by—they cannot harm us
  Where we are sheltered by our Fortress Rock.

Sometimes, perhaps, the ferns may long to blossom,
  Even as we to see our work's reward,
Impatient of the stillness and the shadow,
  Envy the roses on the sunny sward.

"Foolish!" we say, "the dust and heat would kill
    them,
  That sweet, cool shadow is their very life."
Yes—and, God knows, perhaps our spirits' beauty,
  Might, like them, wither in the great world's
    strife.

So He doth keep us, set apart in shadow,
  Far from the lovely gardens' sunny sod;
And why He does it we shall know hereafter.
  "Be still," He says, "I am thy loving God."

Can we not trust our loving heavenly Father
  To do the very best that can be done,
Though one be planted in the glowing sunlight,
  Set in the silence and the shadow—one?

Be we content to say our word in secret,
  Content to wear our garb of sober green,
And, while the world is praising other workers,
  Our tiny seeds cast out, though all unseen.

We may not show our love and zeal by labor,
  Our hands are folded, though they tire of rest;
Fettered the feet that fain would run His errands,
  Willing and swift. But yet, He knoweth best.

Just the conditions which will suit our growing,
  Just the environment we best may stand;
For the green ferns the cool depths of the forest,
  And for our shade the "shadow of His Hand."

The Royal Chamber

WHEN, long ago, some prince made royal
          progress,
       His father's couriers before him sped,
That he might find, where'er he paused for resting,
   A chamber furnished and a banquet spread;
With priceless tapestries the walls were covered,
   With softest carpets all the floors were laid,
And white-robed choir-boys, swinging fragrant
      censers,
   Along his path their sweetest music made;
All lovely harmonies of sound and color,
   That could the ear entrance, the eye delight,
Were made to deck the place of his sojourning,
   Though he should tarry but a day and night.

So we, the children of a royal Father,
   Find in our journeyings a table spread,
For us the splendor of the grass and flowers,
   A carpet fair for pilgrim feet to tread,
For us with tapestries of green and scarlet
   The forest aisles and mountain walls are hung;
For us the music of the winds and waters
   And hymns celestial by the wild birds sung;
For us the glory of the arching heavens,
   Spangled with stars or flushed with rosy light;
So hath He decked the place of our sojourning,
   Though we shall tarry but a day and night.

When the Birds Build

HEAR the chorus that the birds are singing:
  Oh, the skies are blue!
From the Sunny South their flight now wing-
    ing;
  Oh, the skies are blue!
To begin again their happy, happy questing
Till they find a place that suits them for their
      nesting;
Elm-tree, chestnut, maple, there's no telling—
  Oh, the skies are blue!—
Where they'll choose to build their airy dwelling
  Oh, the skies are blue!
Apple-trees are white and pink and growing pinker
Every honey-bee has turned a drinker,
    Oh, the skies are blue!

Blackbird, oriole,—a saucy fellow!
  Oh, the skies are blue!—
In his dashing suit of black and yellow;
  Oh, the skies are blue!
Wren and swallow and the crimson-breasted robin
Wings a-flutter and their little heads a-bobbin',
Sticks and straw from every corner looting,—
  Oh, the skies are blue!—
Send from tree to tree their cheery fluting,
  Oh, the skies are blue!
Every throat, from bobolink to tiny linnet,
Bubbling over with the music in it;
  Oh, the skies are blue!

The Gray Days of November

THE gray days of November
  No plaint from me shall win;
  I shut the fog and mist all out,
And shut the fire-shine in;
I draw my chair the closer
  To where its warm glow cheers,
And, dreaming in the firelight,
  Dream back across the years.

No happier days, no better,
  My lost youth gave to me,
With flowers in every meadow
  And songs from every tree;
That was the time of growing;
  This is the time of rest;
Bloom falls, but fruiting follows,
  And each in turn is best.

God giveth of His glory
  An ever-changing view;
The old things pass forever;
  He maketh all things new;
Life knoweth here no beauty
  That shall not fade away;
Some better things He sendeth,
  And these are mine to-day.

Mine is the riper wisdom
  That comes with graying hair;
Mine is the fuller knowledge
  Of God's great love and care;
Mine is the clearer vision;
  Mine is the wider view;
And mine the hoarded memories
  Of friendships kind and true.

Mine is a steadier patience
 To bear the ills of life;
Mine is a sturdier courage
 To meet the daily strife;
Mine is a faith serener
 Than ever youth could know
To walk the way appointed
 Through sunshine or through snow.

The gray days lead to white days
 Of peace and silence deep,
A stiller hush of resting
 When Earth and I shall sleep;
And then—a glorious waking
 When broken ties all mend.
Through gray days of November
 I wait the long year's end.

The Unbought Good

WHAT would our land be worth to us,—
 The land we sell and buy,
 And fence about, and call our own,
Without God's open sky
To hold the sunset's rose and gold,
 The white clouds floating high?

What would our fields bring forth for us
 Without the gifts He sends,—
Without the sunshine and the rain
 On which our bread depends,
His little water-brooks to flow,
 His birds to be our friends?

Oh, as the land without the sky
 That ever bends above,
So barren and so desolate
 Our lives without His love;
The blessings that no gold can buy
 Our greatest riches prove.

The River's Lullaby

WHEN the evening shadows chase away the
light,
    And the golden sunbeams fade before the
night,
Flows a quiet river, broad and calm and free;
Hear it softly singing, "Come! oh, come with me,
To the Sleepy Harbor, far and far away,
Where, when day is over, all the children stay;
There a lovely country waits thy loitering feet—
'Tis the Baby's Dreamland, fair and bright and
    sweet!"
Sway the tangled rushes, float the silver lilies,
Bend the trailing willows o'er the rippling stream;
Listen, baby, listen to the river's singing—
Let its music mingle with thy peaceful dream.

Gently will the river bear thee on its breast;
Stars will light my darling to the land of rest,
Short and safe the journey,—sleep, and that is all;
"Hasten, baby, hasten," hear the river call;
"Fairies wait thy coming, lovely tales to tell,
And the flower bells' chiming on the wind will swell;
Green are all the meadows for thy tiny feet,
And above thee watches an angel fair and sweet."
Sway the tangled rushes, float the silver lilies,
Bend the trailing willows o'er the rippling stream;
Listen, baby, listen to the river's singing—
Let its music mingle with thy peaceful dream.

Index

Apple Blossoms 27
Christmas Roses 45
Forget-Me-Nots 31
From Forest to Fender 46
How to Tell a Comet 41
In February 11
In the Beginning 3
In the Winter Woods 30
Morning Glories 21
My Trees 42
Nature's Shut-Ins 50
Spring Song of Praise 17
The Bird's Message 14
The Bridge Builders 15
The Butterfly 18
The Camp Fire 23
The Crag of the Cross 34
The Creator 4
The First Song-Sparrow 16
The Flight of the Air-Ship . . . 32
The Gray Days of November . . . 54
The Holly Tree 20
The Little Birds of God 10
The Lullaby of Rain 28
The Making of the Beautiful . . . 6
The Moon 33
The Phoebe Bird 9
The River's Lullaby 56
The Robin's Note 37
The Royal Chamber 52
The Sea Shell 22
The Song of Creation 26
The Song of Running Water . . . 38
The Unbought Good 55
The Water Lily's Story 24
The Winter Birds 44
This is the Day 25
Tom Thumb Yellowbird 8
When Sir Oriole Comes 13
When The Birds Build 53
When The Leaves Fall 12